# MEL
# GIBSON

# MEL GIBSON

## BY

## NEIL SINYARD

**Crescent Books**

New York/Avenel, New Jersey

This 1993 edition published by
Crescent Books,
distributed by Outlet Book Company, Inc.,
a Random House Company,
40 Engelhard Avenue
Avenel, New Jersey 07001

Produced by
Brompton Books Corporation
15 Sherwood Place
Greenwich, CT 06830

ISBN 0-517-06707-2

8 7 6 5 4 3 2 1

Printed and bound in Hong Kong

PREVIOUS PAGES: *Mel Gibson
in a variety of incarnations.
From left,* Air America, Mad Max,
Hamlet *and* Lethal Weapon.

RIGHT: *As Fletcher Christian
in* The Bounty.

# CONTENTS

# INTRODUCTION

There are, thought Orson Welles, some people whom the film camera just seems to love. Mel Gibson is one of those people. When he looks in a mirror, he says, he wonders what all the fuss is about. But when he looks into a camera, a transformation takes place. He is indeed a photographer's dream. 'Mel works under any light,' affirmed the cameraman on *Mad Max 2*, Dean Semler. 'You can put him under fluorescent lighting and he still looks a million dollars.'

Part of the secret of his success is his 'look'. Physically he is not exceptional, being under six foot and not especially muscular or athletic. But he has pale blue eyes that photograph luminously and seem to irradiate the screen. 'Have you noticed,' said the great American director, Anthony Mann (famous for such classic westerns as *Winchester 73, The Naked Spur* and *The Man from Laramie*), 'that all the famous, much admired screen stars have bright eyes – Gary Cooper, Charlton Heston, Henry Fonda, James Stewart, John Wayne, Clark Gable, Burt Lancaster, Robert Taylor, Kirk Douglas, Peter O'Toole. The look does everything: it is a permanent reflection of the inner 'flame' that animates these heroes. An actor who does not have this 'look' can never get beyond background roles'. Mann could have added Paul Newman and Steve McQueen to that list, for it is in that kind of company Gibson belongs and that kind of tradition of which he is a continuation. He has McQueen's kinetic charisma; he also has something of Newman's more laid-back, ironic, introspective persona and, given Gibson's theatrical background and histrionic ambition, potentially Newman's dramatic range, which is an exciting prospect indeed.

There are other distinctive features which have contributed to Gibson's dramatic aura.

Like Paul Newman again, he has an infectious, winning smile that he has traded on very skilfully in his films. Most of his most memorable screen characters have a goofiness to their nature that sometimes takes the other protagonists – and even the audience – by surprise, and he is not above outrageous clowning even during the duel scene in *Hamlet*. Curiously though, when casting Hamlet, the director Franco Zeffirelli said the thing which most immediately drew him to Mel Gibson was his voice – warm and mellifluous. But there was something else: a deeper enigma. 'He's the most interesting young actor of his period,' says Zeffirelli, 'with a mystery that triggers your curiosity. He never really lets himself go.'

The mystery is perhaps less immediately apparent than his sex appeal. Some of his most glowing reviews have come not from the critics but from his co-stars. 'The most gorgeous man I have ever seen,' said Sigourney Weaver, his leading lady in *The Year of Living Dangerously* (1983). Diane Keaton, who played opposite Gibson in the title role of *Mrs. Soffel* (1984), waxed a little more philosophical, calling Mel 'a real well of feelings, a deep core. It was not difficult for me to imagine what it was like to be hopelessly in love with Mel. It was wonderful for me to play opposite him. I didn't have any idea how much emotional range he had.' Perhaps the romantic mystique has been heightened by the fact that he has made no secret that he is a dedicated family man, married to an ex-nurse, Robyn, who, with their six children (Hannah, twins Christian and Edward, Will, Louis and Milo) accompanies him wherever he goes. He seems to like and respect women – 'They're smart, you know,' he once said, 'they understand and see things that men simply don't see' – which makes it easier for those feelings to be reciprocated. Magnetism

RIGHT: *Gibson possesses the kind of magnetic blue eyes that have advanced the careers of many successful actors.*

6

coupled with sensitivity is a pretty devastating combination.

Yet Zeffirelli is right: there is a mysteriousness and duality about his character and screen persona. He was almost an instant star – in only two of his films has he not received top billing – and won a best actor award from the Australian Film Institute with only his third film, *Tim* (1979). Yet for years he tended to shy away from interviews in self-conscious confusion, because he thought he said only silly things or felt a responsibility to be brutally honest, something which occasionally got him into trouble. (Perhaps the most famous occasion was when he unwisely – and indeed unjustly – opined that *Mad Max 3: Beyond Thunderdome* was 'shit'). But ask him about a certain attractive 'feminine' vulnerability in his acting, and he will respond with a fulsome Shakespearian quotation to suggest that this was always part of his character and not in the least influenced by the feminist revolution: 'As Edmund says in *King Lear*, "I should have been that I am had the maidenliest star in the firma-

ment twinkled on my bastardizing."' Those critics who scoffed at the notion of action-man Mel Gibson as Hamlet – 'the biggest part on earth, jointly with Jesus,' as Franco Zeffirelli has put it – should perhaps have recalled that Gibson had more experience of playing Shakespeare than had, for example, Marlon Brando when he took on the role of Antony in Joseph L. Mankiewicz's celebrated *Julius Caesar* (1953). Gibson had not only played Romeo to Judy Davis's Juliet on stage for the State Theatre Company of South Australia, but had even played Titania, Queen of the Fairies in *A Midsummer Night's Dream* when at drama school in Sydney. 'When you have a mask on – you can do almost anything,' he has said. But what lies behind that mask?

If there is a duality in Gibson, the reason is probably that he spent the first 12 years of his life in America, but then his formative adolescent years in Australia, during which he particularly remembers being taunted for being a Yank. 'I was brought up in one environment until about the age of 12 and understood it,' he

has said. 'Then I was suddenly shifted to another. I could immediately sense the difference in, for instance, the extent to which people expressed themselves. Americans, you know, are very expressive, which I think is better than the uptight reserve the Australians have . . . But as with everything it has its good and bad sides. I'll never be a part of either culture fully. But it doesn't bother me – it's good to have a duality.' The American side of Gibson (the religious, success-oriented aspect of America) might be reflected in his staunch, indeed conservative Catholicism, and his ambitious cultivation of his career. The Australian side (sceptical, sacrilegious) shows itself more in the occasional outbursts against, and retreats from, his 'showbiz' lifestyle.

Something of that duality has been caught in the roles he has played, which has added an important dimension to the characters. Behind the charm is a lot of toughness. 'Mel has a lot of anger and hostility,' director Richard Donner (who has done the *Lethal Weapon* films with Gibson) has said, 'He's a real tough son-of-a-bitch underneath. I've seen him come to the edge, seen the pot start to boil and I know to back off and get others to back off.' There might be a strong reservoir of reserve and control in Gibson, but his films have very often taken him to the point of extremity and hyste-

ria. 'You don't get a good story unless there is some kind of evil . . . ,' he has said, but the interesting thing is that the evil is sometimes not outside, but inside, the main character. Gibson emphasized this once in an interview when he made what at the time seemed an unlikely comparison between his *Lethal Weapon* hero and *Hamlet*. 'Good guys and bad guys, it's been the same since *Hamlet*. What the hell's the difference?' he asked, bridling at a questioner who had thought the character and ethics of his *Lethal Weapon* hero a little dubious, to say the least. 'Hamlet goes in and kills people because they did something to him. He's a vigilante.'

Maybe this is the key to Gibson's duality, and even popularity: his creation of a hero who is also an anti-hero, teetering on the brink. He has therefore both the pull of a classic screen hero like Clark Gable and the occasional abrasiveness of a modern rebel like Clint Eastwood. There has often been a dimension of madness in his screen persona: from *Mad Max* to *Hamlet* via *Lethal Weapon* is a very logical route, when one comes down to it. There is even a common cause for this craziness and inner violence. These heroes have been unhinged by the violent destruction of their family lives and by the death of their wives and/or other loved ones. If Gibson gives this aspect of the charac-

BELOW: *Gibson as Dale McKussic, a retired drug dealer, in* Tequila Sunrise.

ter a strong element of authenticity and poignancy, one can surmise that he is drawing, in Stanislavski fashion, on his own feelings about family life, on his own self-awareness, for the key to his performance.

Whatever the inspiration for his characters (and one can feel a similar duality tearing at the 'pragmatic coward' he plays in *Gallipoli* or the tortured figure he makes out of Fletcher Christian in the film of *The Bounty*), he has become the most resonant romantic outsider of current mainstream film. He is currently the screen's blue-eyed boy of crazed competence, com-

mitment and even compassion. What Newman and McQueen stood for in the 1960s – a kind of attractively anarchic abandon – Gibson has represented in the 1980s. *Hamlet* has presented him with a new challenge, and the precise impact of this Everest of acting roles has not yet been fully registered. Will it radically alter the direction of his screen career? What is certain is that it does not affect the validity of Zeffirelli's thumbnail explanation for Gibson's momentous movie popularity and success thus far. 'He is a consummate film actor,' explains Zeffirelli simply, 'and a red-blooded male.'

ABOVE: *A lighthearted moment on the set of* The Bounty. *This was just one of three films Mel made in 1984, and the strain is beginning to show.*

## CHAPTER 1

# LIVING DANGEROUSLY

'**W**hen I started out acting,' Gibson has said, 'I had a suspicion this stardom could happen, but that was all. I didn't care – I mean I *really* didn't care. I had no commitments. But in a funny way, the less you care, the easier you seem to get there.' The apparent effortlessness of his rise to stardom is one of the most extraordinary features of his career. It came without his seeming to have to strain for it, and even without any real prior preparation or planning. It was not as if being a big movie star had ever been a burning ambition. As a child, he would go to the movies and watch Humphrey Bogart and imagine himself as that kind of personality and star. 'But I never took it seriously', he said. 'I never really thought it would happen.' When it did, it took him quite unawares.

Gibson was born in Peekskill, New York in January 1956. His father was a railway brakeman and his mother an ex-opera singer, and Mel one of a family of 11 children. He was brought up as a strict Roman Catholic and educated at St Leo's Christian Brothers School in Sydney. Questioned about his religious beliefs recently, he said, 'I don't go to church anymore because the institution itself has become really corrupt. I'd probably go if I could find the right sort of church because . . . hell, you need it.' He has what one might call conservative views on issues such as capital punishment and gun control and, like his father, is critical of what he sees as the more lax, liberal leanings of Pope John Paul II. When pointedly asked if he shared his father's 'extreme' views in a *Time Out* interview, he retorted: 'I share them because I believe them to be true.'

When Gibson was 12, his father, fearing that his sons were reaching an age that made them eligible to be drafted to Vietnam, decided to use money awarded for an industrial injury to transport his family to Australia. It was a traumatic experience for the boy and he remembers the early years in his new country as being especially difficult. 'I was a very, very timid sort of kid,' he has said, 'but played up like a bastard on the side.' Maybe this playing a role on the outside to cover up the uncertainty within is the thing that developed and nurtured his appetite as an actor. Certainly in his films, the kind of scene that he carries off most strikingly – threatening the South African villains in *Lethal Weapon 2*, or the duel scene or play-acting episode in *Hamlet* – is one in which the character seeks to hide an overwhelming emotion under the cloak of a manic, clownish exterior. When Gibson smiles in a film is often the time when he is at his most dangerous.

Yet the initiative for his acting career came not from himself, but from his sister. Unbeknown to him, she sent off an application to the National Insitute of Dramatic Art in Sydney. 'When she told me she had done it,' Mel has said, 'I didn't really go for it much, but then I sat down and said, "Well, why not? Why not two days out of my life?" But I felt I was going to make a jerk of myself in front of a lot of people.' Yet he found the experience very valuable. The trick was, he found, to be open to every new experiment, in the expectation that you could enjoy it for itself and in the hope that it might be useful in developing new skills. So he did gymnastics, which certainly stood him in good stead for the role of the young runner in *Gallipoli* and for the physical nature of his later roles. He did fencing, which is a handy accomplishment for any prospective Hamlet. And he also willingly tried out a variety of unlikely roles ('they deliberately miscast you') which he enjoyed enormously. Ever since there has always

RIGHT: *Franco Zeffirelli has called Gibson 'the consummate film actor,' a compliment he has lived up to with a wide variety of roles.*

Nightrider. But Nightrider's successor, Toe-cutter and his equally malevolent partner, Johnny, wage a vendetta against Max, killing his closest cop buddy and preying on his family, in the process of which Max's wife is maimed and his son run over. Max in turn will pursue his vengeance against the bike gang until only Johnny is left. Manacled, and with a huge fire about to ignite, Johnny is offered one chance of survival by his enemy: he can go free if he saws through his leg with the hacksaw which Max has kindly provided.

Researching the film for locations (and the setting is very expressively used, the harsh wilderness seeming an effective correlative to the bleak emotions), Kennedy had come into contact with a host of road accident victims who had survived crashes but had remained traumatized as a result of their experience. The road as a site of danger, and the car or bike as both thrill machine and lethal weapon are concepts that feed into the film. *Mad Max* can be seen as a sci-fi critique of the role of the car in our culture. Director George Miller had studied medicine and worked as a doctor while making short films prior to *Mad Max*, and he summarized the theme of the film as 'a cautionary comment on unsafe driving which as an MD I have had to treat.' After viewing one sequence, fellow director Richard Franklin, maker of such stylish thrillers as *Patrick* and *Roadgames*, remarked prophetically to Miller: 'You're going to be very rich one day.' The film was a tearaway commercial success.

'It has all the moral uplift of *Mein Kampf*,' wrote Philip Adams, who was to become the chairman of the Australian Film Commission. In some quarters the violence was deplored and, as with *Dirty Harry*, the film was seen by some as being ethically dubious, seeming to endorse Max's vigilante violence when more orthodox legal channels had been blocked. It is a fun film, an anarchic comic-strip that whips up its elements into a goulash of gore, Gothicism and grotesquerie. What was intriguing to audiences of the time, though, was its contribution to relatively uncharted genre territory – i.e. Australian science fiction, and its vision of the future as a new dark age, in which modern civilization was not only stagnant but provided weaponry against itself and dismantled its development. The new society imagined here was not going back to the future but forward to the past, towards a new dawn of barbarism. It offered not simply the survival of the fittest but survival of the fascist.

Legend has it – and it seems as far removed from reality as Mad Max himself – that Mel Gibson landed the role because he turned up for the audition with a bruise from a fight in a pub. He actually got the part because he established an immediate rapport with the director ('there is no one who can surpass him in that style,' he was to comment later on George Miller) and

seemed to be an injection of playfulness in Gibson's acting. As an actor, whatever the role, he usually seems to be having a good time.

Even when only a student, the roles started coming. He played the role of a naval officer ('I inspected navels') in the soap opera, *The Sullivans*, which he described as 'a shocking experience – terrible scripts, no rehearsals, just knock it over in a day. I did two weeks' work and I was on the screen every night for three weeks.' He also appeared in a low-budget surfing movie, *Summer City* (1976), in which he played an inarticulate surfer called Scollop and for which he was paid 20 dollars. But at the end of his second years at NIDA, something altogether more exciting came up: an audition for a role in an inexpensive action movie that had something of the flavor of Roger Corman's biker movies of the 1960s and had all the potential of a cult hit. It was called *Mad Max*.

*Mad Max* (1979) was essentially the brainchild of two people new to the cinema, producer Byron Kennedy and director George Miller. It is a sort of futuristic *Dirty Harry*. Max Rockatansky (Gibson) is the star member of the police force, or Main Force Patrol as it is called. Max has recently caused the death of the psychopathic leader of a motorcycle gang,

ABOVE AND LEFT: Mad Max, *made in 1980, is now something of a cult movie. It was made on an extremely low budget, but nevertheless ensured Gibson's recognition as an Antipodean star.*

because he could convey exactly the kind of charisma and sense of caricature that the part required. Presence was more important than performance. Gibson found it fun to do, recognizing that the character was cardboard and cartoon-like and relishing the challenge of having to integrate his performance into the film's comic-book style while still maintaining sympathy and conviction. The other challenge for the actor was Max's nature as 'a closet human being', as Gibson put it. 'He has to interact with other characters,' said Gibson, 'and yet at the same time not appear to.'

If *Mad Max* established Gibson as an action-man star in his adopted country (international recognition would come later), his next film was to establish him as a soulful romantic leading man, a junior league Montgomery Clift. He played the title role in *Tim* (1979), a part which was to reward him with the best actor award from the Australian Film Institute. Based on the first novel by *Thorn Birds* author Colleen McCullough, *Tim* is basically the story of an unlikely romance between a 40-year-old businesswoman (Piper Laurie) and a simple-minded but handsome handyman (Mel

Gibson) who comes to help her. Against all the odds, the film almost works, largely due to the sensitive playing of the principals, and the equally fine performances from Alwyn Kurts and Patricia Evison as Tim's parents. (Kurts and Evison also won Australian Film Institute awards as best supporting actor and actress, respectively).

Unfortunately, the film is weighted down by Eric Jupp's sugary score, which sounds like John Barry on an off day; and by director Michael Pate's funereal pacing of the material that seems to take its tempo from the laboriousness of Tim's thought-processes. The main problem is the basic sentimentality of its conception which the film unwittingly highlights through its inclusion of a brief, realistic scene at an actual school for the mentally retarded.

Gibson's next film, *Attack Force Z* (1980), was something of a disaster. It had a change of title, originally being called *The Z Men*. Prob-ably more damagingly, it also had a last-minute change of director, the imaginative Phil Noyce (director of *Newsfront* and later stylish thrillers such as *Heatwave* and *Dead Calm*) being replaced by the dependable hack Tim Burstall. Something of that sense of chaos and confusion is apparent in the final film. It is based on the activities of an actual unit operating in the southwest Pacific in World War Two. The specific opening caption – 10 January, 1945 – seems to herald a certain authenticity. What follows, though, in this story of a mission to rescue a Japanese scientist whose knowledge might shorten the war, is a dismal catalog of weary action scenes, a dreary love story, overcute kids and an undercooked script of the 'There's only one way to find out' variety.

It has a strong cast, the members of the mission including Gibson, Sam Neill, Chris Haywood, John Waters (who, no doubt gratefully, does not survive beyond the opening ten minutes) and, for international appeal, John

BELOW: *Mel Gibson and Piper Laurie won Australian Film Institute awards for their sensitive portrayal of an unlikely romance in* Tim.

Philip Law. As these interlopers wander around an exotic terrain on an obscure mission which no one understands, endangering the lives of the native inhabitants, one suspects at times a tentative Vietnam allegory. 'Are you Americans?' they are asked as they blunder into the area. A harsh view of war is occasionally suggested by the futility of the mission and by imagery which is sometimes brutal (a harmless old man, who inadvertently witnesses the arrival of the task force, is shot offscreen) sometimes bizarre (a Chinese festival that seems designed to ward off evil Japanese aggressors) and sometimes both brutal and bizarre (the heroine being tortured in her own noodle soup). Mainly, though, it seems more like *The Magnificent Seven* in the Pacific, as a small band of heroic men come to the aid of villagers fighting a ruthless enemy.

Mel Gibson plays a captain who, it is implied, is too young and inexperienced for his rank. A comment perhaps on Gibson's meteoric rise to stardom? Characteristically, Gibson's response in this role is not one of resentment or bravado, but of sensitivity and vulnerability. He is not afraid to show the character's weaknesses – his jumpiness, his indecision. He makes promises, but can he keep them? 'You think I'm making a mess of this,' he says to Sam Neill, who denies it: certainly Gibson is making no more of a mess than anyone else in the film, including the director. The film is almost more interesting for what it has to re-

veal about Gibson's potential than for what it has to say about his character, or about war, for that matter. He has promise, but can he live up to it? The film's conviction of his star status is mainly signaled by the fact that, of the main cast characters, he is the only one who is allowed to survive.

Gibson was to play a survivor in his next film, also a war movie, though there the comparison with *Attack Force Z* mostly ends. One of Australian cinema's mightiest epics, Peter Weir's *Gallipoli* (1981) culminates in one of the bloodiest episodes of World War One in which thousands of young Australian and New Zealand soldiers perished. The film is indignant about insensitive military blundering but believes that too many atrocities have been committed in the name of being 'anti-war' for this to be the primary purpose of the film. It is concerned instead to examine and understand the misplaced enthusiasm which drew so many young men to this battle. To this end, it particularly explores the friendship between two combatants, the farmboy, Archie (Mark Lee), and a more worldly drifter, Frank Dunn (Gibson).

Both are exceptional sprinters, who meet for the first time when competing against each other on the athletics track. There are inevitable echoes of Hugh Hudson's *Chariots of Fire* (1981), but the tone of the two films is very different, the nostalgic imperialism celebrated by the latter being precisely the quality that leads

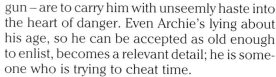

to the holocaust in *Gallipoli*. Significantly, the athletics imagery of *Gallipoli* becomes increasingly menacing. Races against time, presented as chivalrous and even jokey encounters on the athletics field, become a matter of life and death on the battlefield. Clocks and watches there become instruments as lethal as machine guns since successful strategy is all a matter of timing. Archie's legs – 'steel springs' as he calls them, an image that eerily evokes parts of both the watch and the

gun – are to carry him with unseemly haste into the heart of danger. Even Archie's lying about his age, so he can be accepted as old enough to enlist, becomes a relevant detail; he is someone who is trying to cheat time.

There are similar details in the earlier part of the film which seem inessential but assume a larger significance and testify to the structural sophistication of David Williamson's screenplay. A recruiting drive interrupts an athletics meeting early on in a manner that anticipates the fusion of athleticism and the military in the film's tense finale, when the fate of a whole company is to depend on the speed at which Frank can run (he is carrying a vital message). A humorous scene, when the young Australians poke fun at British military arrogance, takes on a darker perspective later when the same kind of military pomposity callously puts these young men's lives at risk.

There is some neat satire on Australian insularity. At one stage Frank and Archie meet an old-timer who materializes out of the Australian desert (significantly, Archie's watch, a gift from his uncle which he has used as a compass for navigation, has led them astray) and who does not even know there is a war on in Europe. The attitude the man embodies explains the eagerness of Australian youths to enlist. They wish to have something more than just an impression of the outside world. Gallipoli, which they can hardly pronounce, is not so much a place as an idea. They see it as a

challenge to their manhood and a promise of exotic adventure. The first shot of the battle area is unforgettable, seen at night through an unearthly blue mist with its mysterious lights giving it the appearance, as Weir has said, of a ghostly funfair.

As the friendship between Archie and Frank develops, so does the contrast between them. The impact of the war on Frank brings out his dogged will simply to survive, while the blond Archie is given the archaic nobility of a romantic, viewing the conflict as 'an adventure somehow larger than life.' The final scene shows Frank running parallel to the battle while Archie is running straight into it, his dreams of adventure and his uncle's Kipling-esque invocation to 'be a man', about to blow up in his face. These are eloquent images for Frank's defensive irony and Archie's headlong heroism.

Gibson always insisted that his character was a pragmatist not a coward, and with a really strong survival instinct. 'There are guys who say "I'm no coward; I'd go out and die for the country" and do. Frank didn't. He had flashes of bravery but only when there was no other choice.' It is once again a sensitive performance, a hero believably flawed, human rather than obviously heroic. Already a kind of duality was becoming apparent in his screen persona, as he seemed able to switch between a virile and vulnerable masculinity. Interestingly, and tellingly, although it is Mark Lee who makes all the heroic gestures and dies nobly in a striking final tableau, it is Gibson who steals the film, with his more rounded humanity and

21

more compelling charisma. It is a star performance. Just as the film is about a movement away from 'reality', from a character's Australian roots to a mysterious outside world, so Gibson's performance suggests a screen presence about to burst beyond its national boundaries. It is a performance that won him a second Australian Film Institute award as best actor, the Institute rewarding the film with six other awards (film, director, photography, screenplay, sound, editing).

*Gallipoli* had been produced by a new company formed by Rupert Murdoch and Robert Stigwood. The latter's connections with Paramount ensured its world-wide release. The original, rather unfortunate publicity slogan ('From the place you've never heard of . . . the story you'll never forget . . . ') had to be changed to 'a place you *may* never have heard of . . .' Nevertheless, its international distribution and acclaim helped make it the most successful Australian film up to that date, and

BELOW: The Road Warrior, *the second* Mad Max *film, brought Gibson's charms to an international audience.*

brought Mel Gibson to the attention of a much larger public than ever before. His next film was the one that clinched his stardom and, as he put it, 'made the US look at me.' The film was *Mad Max 2* (1981).

'In the roar of an engine he lost everything . . . and became a shell of a man . . . a burnt out desolate man, a man haunted by the demons of his past . . . a man who wandered out into the Waste Land . . . And it was here, in this blighted place, that he learned to live again.' So states the portentous Prologue, endeavoring to evoke and anticipate the mythical status of the film's

hero; briefly summarize what has gone before; and prepare us for the desolate civilization that awaits. Predators are prowling around in a post-third world war environment, searching for petrol which has become the world's most valuable property. Mad Max learns of a petrol refinery but discovers that the community there, led by Pappagallo, is under siege by the masked giant Humungus and his bike warriors. Max contrives to steal a juggernaut that will tow Pappagallo's petrol tanker to the safety of 'Paradise' (a former holiday resort), and a running battle ensues when the convoy makes its bid for freedom, chased by the bikers.

Entitled *The Road Warrior* in America, *Mad Max 2* has been described by the eminent Australian critic David Stratton, as 'virtually a cowboys-and-indians western in a new guise'. Pappagallo's people are the cavalry defending the fort and the bikers are the marauding savages. Alternatively Pappagallo's people are the homesteaders and the bikers are the ruthless cattlemen who are trying to force them off their land. *Mad Max 2* has something of the structure of a futuristic, sci-fi *Shane*. Like Shane, Max is almost a mythical figure, with a

ABOVE: *Max (with an expression that truly emphasizes the epithet 'mad') saves the Feral Kid (Emil Minty) from the wild bikers.*

psychological wound, and who comes from nowhere to help a community in trouble. When the job is done, he will disappear as mysteriously as he came. Like the film *Shane* (although the identity of the narrator is not revealed until the end), the narrative is partly seen through the eyes of an adoring youngster, the Feral Kid (Emil Minty). 'This was the last we ever saw of him,' he says of the road Warrior as he disappears into the desert. 'He lives now only in my memories.'

*Shane* is not the only reference point of the

film. Director George Miller has said he was particularly influenced by Joseph Campbell's book about Jungian mythology, *The Hero With a Thousand Faces*, which had such a profound effect on George Lucas when conceiving the *Star Wars* sagas. The mythic quality of Max – the importance of the psychological wound, the purifying violence, the manner in which he lives on in the memory of those who encountered him – owes much to this source. The film also has something of the rough humor and raw vitality of Kurosawa in his *Yojimbo* (1961) mood, a reference reinforced by the use of a very Kurosawa-like stylistic device of horizontal wipes, and by the depiction of a hero who, on the point of death, seems to rise again. It has also some of Kurosawa's style of black comedy. 'Look at you,' a battered Max is told. 'You couldn't even drive a wheelchair.' The remarkable stunt work has the comic-book panache of a psychopathic *Raiders of the Lost Ark*. The first *Mad Max* had been dubbed into rather atrocious American for its international release, but in this version, Miller seems positively to accentuate its attitudes of Aussie anarchy. Nothing conveys this better than the beloved boomerang, symbol of the national culture, which here is an instrument murderous enough to slice off the fingers of anyone unwise enough to catch it and which winds up

buried in the skull of the chief villain's blond boyfriend.

Amid such fury and frenzy, it takes a powerful acting presence to make itself felt at all. Like Harrison Ford in the Indiana Jones films, Gibson manages to rise above the gadgetry to convey something of the personality beneath. His facial expression when a music box plays 'Happy Birthday to You' is hauntingly eloquent, reined in, but suggesting a flickering memory of family life and domestic humanity that has been all but erased in his brutal struggle for survival. Because Miller is very skilful at playing off Max's withdrawn character against the manic bravado of Bruce Spence's aviator or against a context of humor (such as the shot of the dog's disappointment as Max unconcernedly devours a tin of dog food), the power of Gibson's persona of brooding stoicism comes through very forcefully. With his motorbike, blue eyes, babyish face, enigmatic smile and the ability to move from the kind of stillness at the center of a hurricane to bravura energy and violence that seem to crackle like an electric storm, Gibson had never looked more like a new Steve McQueen.

ABOVE: *The Road Warrior himself; Mel Gibson at his most electrifying.*

The setting of Gibson's next film thrust him not into a post-holocaust wasteland but the politically combustible territory of Indonesia in 1965. *The Year of Living Dangerously* (1983) reunited him with director Peter Weir, who also co-wrote the screenplay with David Williamson and the author of the original novel, C.J. Koch. Somewhat underrated at the time, it now looks like one of Weir's finest films, exploring a characteristic theme of the outsider who is thrown into a new situation that forces him to reassess his values. It also provides one of Gibson's most skilful and thoughtful performances. It was on the basis of this role particularly that Weir declared: 'Mel is the new Australian. He is going to be a very big star. He is quite different from the Australian everyone knows – the kind Rod Taylor represents.'

Gibson plays Guy Hamilton, who arrives in Jakarta on his first foreign assignment with the Australian Broadcasting Service. His welcome from the other Western journalists, who survive in a smokescreen of seedy cynicism as a defense against their unpopularity in the country, is less than friendly. But he is adopted by a hunch-backed dwarf, the photographer Billy Kwan (a remarkable Oscar-winning performance by the American actress, Linda Hunt) who offers to be his 'eyes', introducing him to the city, facilitating the occasional scoop.

More deviously, Billy also engineers a romance between Hamilton and Jill Bryant (Sigourney Weaver), an attaché at the British Embassy.

However, Billy becomes disillusioned with Hamilton when, through Jill, Hamilton learns that the Indonesian Communist party (PKI) is preparing a military coup and waiting for a Chinese arms shipment before launching their assault. He wants to break the story as a major journalistic scoop even though it would damage his romance with Jill, who told it him in confidence: Billy is appalled. A more crushing disillusionment for Billy occurs when the death of a child whom he has been supporting financially destroys his faith in President Sukarno's rule. He stages a public protest that will lead to his death. The final part of the film is an exciting portrayal of the chaos in the city after the failure of the coup and the imposition of martial law. Jill is on a plane to leave. Endeavoring to join her but also protect his driver who is a member of the now outlawed Communist party, Hamilton is badly injured by a palace guard. Should he stay and receive appropriate medical attention for his seriously damaged eye – or should he join Jill at the airport?

Although Gibson plays the main role, for much of the time the narrative is seen through the eyes of Billy, who is the film's observer, nar-

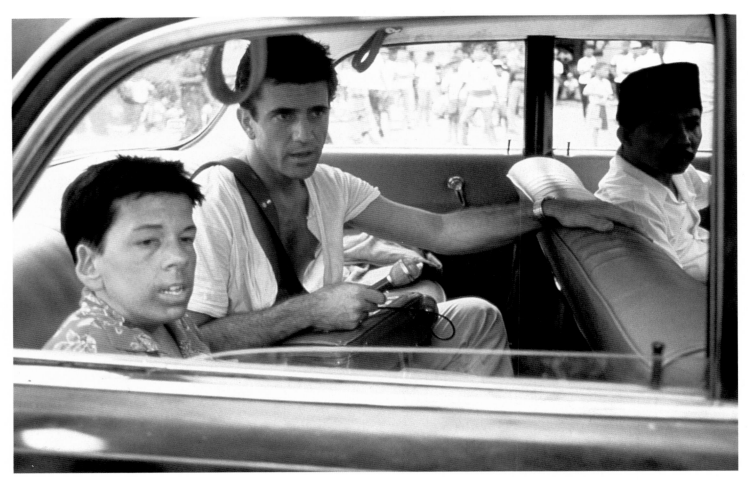

ABOVE: *Guy Hamilton (Gibson) with his guide Billy Kwan (brilliantly portrayed by actress Linda Hunt) in the troubled Indonesia of 1965.*

RIGHT: The Year of Living Dangerously *provided Gibson with one of his more interesting roles, and he produced a taut and skilful performance.*

rator, conscience, political idealist and emotional manipulator. We see shadow puppets over the credits of the film and this becomes, first, a political metaphor for Sukarno, as he manipulates the political forces in his country; and secondly, a personal metaphor for Billy, as he attempts to manipulate the feelings of both Hamilton and Jill. Mel Gibson commented astutely on the film's main theme of manipulation: 'There is the Wayang sacred shadow puppet plays and the way the country was run, neither left nor right but by a delicate balance controlled by Sukarno, the king god. Then there is the same story on a smaller scale with Kwan balancing his puppets: Hamilton, Jill and whoever else is around.' One might also say that the film aims for a delicate balance between penetrating political drama and involving love story.

On the surface, Guy Hamilton might seem to be a thankless role. He is for the most part powerless, a pawn more than a king in the political game. He does not initiate events but is affected by them, a shadowy figure himself, often buffeted by forces he cannot control. He is also rather unscrupulous, seemingly prepared to sacrifice the love of a woman in favor of the big story. He has to be wounded (significantly, in the eye) in order to gain insight into the complicated consequences of his actions and what it is he truly values. Gibson plays him with just the right amount of bewildered charm. At this stage of his career, he portrayed

inexperience very well, being able to communicate vulnerability (one of the things which draws Billy to him) without any sacrifice of masculinity. There is something unformed about Hamilton, something hooded and reserved: the film is about the yearning and the need to live dangerously in emotional as well as political terms. Gibson communicates this wary emotionalism very well.

Perhaps the film is at its best in its depiction of the limited understanding in Western eyes of their cultural and colonialist blunderings, and in showing the gap between Eastern deprivation and Western decadence. The atmosphere of journalistic seediness (with Michael Murphy superb as the devious, debauched American reporter) is powerfully caught. Yet the love story has an erotic charge too, not so much because of the characterization but because of the chemistry of its two stars. Sigourney Weaver's assessment of her leading man as 'gorgeous' was reciprocated by Gibson, who talked warmly of their close friendship and their working rapport. Looks exchanged at a party, a daredevil ride through road blocks, a growing sexual hunger for each other fed as much through the laughter in their relationship as through love – these are all potent elements in their involvement and are passionately conveyed through performance and direction.

In the journal he obsessively keeps, Billy makes an interesting judgment at one stage on

Hamilton: 'Ambitious, self-contained . . . despite your naiveté . . . I sense a potential.' It could almost be a judgment on Mel Gibson himself at this stage. The American critic Pauline Kael noticed in this film that by using his eyes more, that he was bringing 'a spunky romantic comedy quality to the role.' He has never had to try to win over the camera: he can seduce it without trying. Yet sometimes he seems unaware of this power and presence, which could perhaps be energized more. It was a thing he noticed when watching the approach of Linda Hunt and Michael Murphy: they had tons of energy and tension, whereas,

as he put it, 'I usually come in from underneath some place.' He recalls being told by Peter Weir on one occasion: 'You were 15 per cent of what you should be in that shot. You'll get away with it, but be aware of it!' As it happens, this shy, withdrawn quality suits the character of Hamilton, and it comes over as one of Gibson's most subtle screen performances, only to be matched later in this vein by his work in *Mrs Soffel* and *Tequila Sunrise*. Billy might have sensed Hamilton's potential: but in this film, we sense Gibson's own imminent star quality, and his growing development as one of the most effective film actors of his generation.

## CHAPTER 2

# DISH FROM 'DOWN UNDER'

It was inevitable that, sooner or later, and particularly after the smash hit of *Mad Max 2*, Mel Gibson would try his luck in Hollywood. A number of his Australian film compatriots – directors such as Peter Weir, Bruce Beresford, Fred Schepisi and Gillian Armstrong, and actors and actresses like Judy Davis and Bryan Brown – were being lured to America with lucrative offers after their contribution to the resurgence of Australian cinema in the 1970s. Also Gibson seemed to have everything that guaranteed success: good looks, dramatic versatility, and a profound acquaintance with the country. In fact, this career move proved initially to be a little problematical.

For one thing, at this stage as so often in his life, one felt Gibson being torn in two directions. After the culture shock of Australia, he was now having to re-immerse himself in a different, more cut-throat community. He was now ambitious to achieve success as a movie star, yet, as an actor, he got more satisfaction from his stage work. At this time he was playing a variety of stage roles for the State Theatre Company of South Australia in Adelaide, from *Romeo and Juliet* to *Waiting for Godot*. One of his great learning experiences around this time on stage was playing the role of the son Biff to the Willy Loman of that 'bloody good actor' (in Gibson's phrase), Warren Mitchell in Arthur Miller's *Death of a Salesman*. Such variety and opportunity might be harder to come by in America. Then there was the problem of his choice of films – *The Bounty* (1984), *The River* (1984) and *Mrs Soffel* (1984). These were, at the very least, interesting films and, in the last case, probably considerably more than that. But they were not commercially successful. Moreover they did not ease Gibson particularly gently towards international stardom. He had to contend for screen space with some formidable performers: Anthony Hopkins, Sissy Spacek, Diane Keaton. And the choice of roles was quirky and even perverse: a volatile, unstable Fletcher Christian who contrived to make even Captain Bligh look sympathetic; a murderer; and an ineffectual farmer reduced to impotence, and resorting to becoming part of a scab labor force (for which he is spat at) to support his wife and family. They were certainly a varied, challenging set of roles, but suggested that a niche had not yet been found for him, that his screen persona was a bit nebulous.

Then there was the bunching of the films: three arduous film roles in quick succession, to be followed immediately afterwards by *Mad Max 3: Beyond Thunderdome* (1985). 'I wasn't trying to prove anything,' Gibson said later. 'I was just trying to keep busy. Because you don't know what direction you're going in, the best thing to do is just to keep scrambling.' One can sense a certain insecurity underlying that remark. The fact is he was making even Michael Caine look inactive. And Caine has talked of this compulsion to keep working as a kind of insecurity, a kind of terror: if you keep working, you think, maybe they won't notice you are not as good as they seem to think; but if you keep accumulating experience through work, maybe you will *become* that good.

The strain began to tell on Mel. 'He's in danger of blowing it,' said his co-star on *The Bounty*, Anthony Hopkins, 'unless he takes hold of himself.' This was during a time when, according to one report, 'Mel's face was rescued from near catastrophe,' when he was involved in a pub brawl. Later in the year he was put under arrest for drunken driving. The climax was probably in a notorious interview he gave in *People* magazine, when he was labeled 'The Sexiest Man Alive.' He was re-

RIGHT: *In 1984 Mel made his first American film,* The River.

ABOVE: *Gibson at his most gorgeous as Fletcher Christian in* The Bounty.

ported as spitting, swearing, as well as trashing his then current film, *Mad Max 3*. In a state of exhaustion, he resolved to give up drinking and retired to his cattle ranch in New South Wales for a year. He was to return with a bang: *Lethal Weapon* (1987). Although this was a tricky and troubled time in his career, the films he made during it reflect no discredit on him. *The Bounty* (1984) was bound to come in for some adverse criticism, being the third film version of the tale and Gibson's Christian being up against Clark Gable's and Marlon Brando's for comparison. It was also far from being a fresh project in another sense, for a long time being nurtured by director David Lean (with Christopher Reeve as a possible Fletcher Christian) until relations irrevocably broke down between Lean and the producer, Dino de Laurentis. The project was finally put to sea under the helmsmanship of New Zealand

director, Roger Donaldson.

Told in flashback from Bligh's testimony at his court-martial, the story is partly one of broken friendship. The initial friendship between Bligh and Christian is first put under strain by Bligh's rigid and sometimes ruthless seamanship, which alienates Christian. But it comes to a crisis when they stop on the island of Tahiti to deliver their breadfruit plants and Christian becomes intoxicated with the spirit of the place. This island section of the story is very well done. Bligh grows more defiantly disciplinarian as Christian and the crew become more deliriously uninhibited. Natural man begins to surface, and the story becomes almost a precursor of those tales of Joseph Conrad and Graham Greene that watch the processes by which a white man disintegrates in the tropics. The civilized Christian becomes like a painted savage, covered with tattoos,

ABOVE: *Captain Bligh (Anthony Hopkins, seated right) and First Lieutenant Christian (Mel Gibson, seated left) arrive on the tropical island paradise of Tahiti. The very image of stiff upper-lipped naval officers, Bligh and Christian were soon to have their world turned upside down.*

LEFT: The Bounty *leaves Tahiti, a less than happy ship.*

sensually in thrall to a native girl. Bligh reprimands him and, to Christian's cry, 'I have done no more than any natural man would do,' reminds him of the distinction between natural and bestial. Yet Bligh's sense of outrage is also somewhat ambiguous. Is he jealous of Christian, the man's breaking of the bonds of repression, or possibly harboring a repressed desire for Christian himself? Whatever the motives, his horror at Christian's going 'native' poisons the relationship. On the return journey, the conflict between them, coupled with Bligh's hauteur and unyielding regime with his now unruly crew, lead to mutiny.

The mutiny and its aftermath is often the episode where Bligh really comes to dominate the story: it certainly is in the Clark Gable/ Charles Laughton 1935 version. But it is here in the film that Gibson particularly comes into his own. When the mutineers seem to be threaten-

ing to kill Bligh, Christian, in Gibson's hands, completely loses control, hysterically defending the captain whose authority he has just usurped. It is high-risk strategy from the actor, because it takes an audience by surprise and could seem incredible and even ludicrous. Yet Gibson makes it seem not only effective but even moving, as a hollow man suddenly sees the momentousness of what he has done. He tries on the one hand to dignify it (by stopping its degeneration into revenge) but his crazed behavior really discloses his despair: with this one action, he has cut all connections with his former life and must now drift where he will, a lost soul. The film ends with two close-ups: of Anthony Hopkin's Bligh in tears, exonerated at the court-martial; and Mel Gibson's Christian on a bare rock of Pitcairn Island, staring blankly at the limitless sea.

Gibson's first American film was *The River*

ABOVE AND LEFT: *Mel Gibson with Tevaite Vernette, who played his Tahitian lover. The* Bounty *is based on a true story; Christian and other members of the crew were loathe to leave their Tahitian girlfriends behind and it is this that provoked the mutiny. They eventually settled with their womenfolk on the remote Pitcairn Island, which is today inhabited by their descendants.*

FAR LEFT: *Mel Gibson with Sissy Spacek in* The River.

ABOVE: *The Garveys, a struggling smallholding family in Tennessee, were forced to defend their lands against the incursions of local tycoons.*

LEFT: *Mel Gibson as Tom Garvey in* The River. *Having failed to support his family by farming, Garvey has to accept a job as a scab laborer at a local foundry.*

(1984), glossily directed by Mark Rydell, with resplendent photography by Vilmos Zsigmond and an imaginative score by John Williams. In it he plays Tom Garvey, who is a struggling Tennessee smallholder, married to Mae (Sissy Spacek). Farming land that has come down to him through generations, Garvey is having difficulty in making ends meet but stubbornly refuses to sell out to the tycoon Wade (Scott Glen), who wants to dam the river and flood the existing farmland. In desperation, Garvey accepts a temporary job as a scab laborer at a foundry in Birmingham, Alabama, which is both dangerous (he is attacked) and humiliating. Left on her own to look after the farm, Mae also has to resist the romantic overtures of Wade. When the strike ends, Tom must return to face the problems of his farm. The conflict between Nature and Industry is starkly portrayed: Mae is injured by a corn harvester, only managing to free herself by calling on the aid of a charging bull. One of the few moments of light relief during Tom's soul-destroying work at the foundry occurs when a deer wanders into the factory and runs wild and free. One establishing shot of Tom's workplace resembles a vision of hell. The film was one of a roughly contemporary trio of movies – the other two being *Places in the Heart* (1984) and *Country* (1984) – that were implicitly rural protests against Reaganite recession and which, unusually, contrasted their relatively weak emasculated heroes with strong, resourceful heroines – Sally Field in *Places*, Jessica Lange in *Country*. For Gibson, *The River* was an honorable enough American film debut but the part he played – an ineffectual, at one point impotent, scab and potential cuckold – was hardly likely to establish him as the new male heartthrob.

Gibson had only a break of six weeks before starting on his next film, *Mrs. Soffel* (1984). Nevertheless, it probably seemed a more congenial assignment than *The River* for he was working with fellow Australian emigres: director Gillian Armstrong, recruited for the film on the strength of her international success with *My Brilliant Career* (1979); and cinematographer Russell Boyd, who had photographed Mel in *Gallipoli* and *The Year of Living Dangerously*.

Set in turn-of-the-century Pittsburgh in what Gillian Amstrong described as 'an ugly,

tough environment at the beginning of the industrial age,' *Mrs Soffel* is based on a true story. The title character (Diane Keaton) is trapped in an unhappy marriage to the warden of Allegheny County Jail (Edward Herrmann). Her only solace is her family and her religion but the strain of her domestic entrapment, almost in the manner of a Dickens heroine, discloses itself in bouts of hypochondria. On her regular visits of Christian comfort to the jail, she becomes intrigued by the situation of two brothers, Ed and Jack Biddle (Mel Gibson and Matthew Modine, respectively) who have been sentenced to death for the murder of a grocer whose shop they have robbed. Mrs Soffel becomes particularly drawn to Ed, partially because he seems repentant, but mainly because they seem instinctively to recognize that they are both in different kinds of prison. Their mutual attraction leads to a prison break; an escape across snowy Canadian landscapes; a suicide pact as the hunt closes in; and a finale that manages to be alternately tense, tragic and transcendent.

Visually the film is enormously impressive. Russell Boyd's subdued photography emphasizes the claustrophobia of the prison and the oppressive atmosphere of the surrounding industrial landscape, which gives an added frisson when the film itself, as well as the characters, escapes into the pristine whiteness of the exteriors. The final chase is grippingly exciting, building to an image that Gillian Armstrong had in her mind all the time when settling on the photographic texture of the movie:

ABOVE: *Director Gillian Armstrong confers with Mel Gibson and Diane Keaton on the set of* Mrs Soffel.

RIGHT: *Matthew Modine with Gibson and Keaton. Modine and Gibson played two jailbird brothers, helped to freedom by Mrs Soffel.*

FAR RIGHT: *Ed Biddle (Gibson) falls in love with Mrs Soffel (Keaton). Part of the tension in the film hinges on the question of whether their relationship is one of convenience or true feeling.*

ABOVE: Mrs Soffel *is extremely impressive in purely visual terms, the snowy landscape making the final escape scene particularly effective.*

blood on the snow.

The director could not have been more fulsome in her praise for the three leading actors, Keaton, Gibson and Modine. 'They were very professional,' she said, 'working in hideous conditions without complaint.' What she particularly liked about Mel Gibson's performance was the 'duality he put into the role of Ed Biddle.' Is he merely manipulating Mrs Soffel, aware of the effect he is having on her and wondering how to use it to his best advantage; or is he himself being carried on an emotional wave, uncertain of his own feelings until the

point he realizes he himself is in love? 'That was the thing that attracted Mel,' said Armstrong, 'and a lot of other actors who were after that role. That was the great challenge: to play that ambiguity and to identify the point where he changes and the game backfires on him.'

Certainly Gibson and Diane Keaton play excellently together, bringing a spontaneity to their humor and devotion. The American critic Pauline Kael likened Gibson's performance to the young Henry Fonda, thinking no doubt of the doomed romanticism of a film like Fritz Lang's *You Only Live Once* (1937). The love

story ends in tragedy, with Mrs Soffel behind bars, and a social outcast. But the final effect is not tragic. Her love for Ed has released her. She is imprisoned but our final view of her suggests that, in emotional and spiritual terms, she has been liberated.

For all its big studio trappings, *Mrs Soffel* still retained something of the atmosphere, intimacy and raw realism of an independent movie. But it was back to the hardware and special effects for Mel Gibson's next film, *Mad Max 3: Beyond Thunderdome* (1985), another everyday story of post-holocaust survival. The size of the spectacle this time demanded that the film had two directors: George Miller, who took care of the action and the scenes involving the feral children, and George Ogilvie, a stage director, who was assigned to look after the actors.

When robbed of his vehicle by a flying scavenger Jedediah, Mad Max (Gibson) pursues the thief to the growing community of Bartertown, which is run by the local dictator Aunty Entity (Tina Turner) and where everyone and everything is up for sale. Falling foul of the authorities, Max is promised a return of his property if he helps Aunty in her struggle against Master Blaster, who runs Bartertown's underground. They duel to the death in the vast Thunderdome, only for Max to relent when he has his opponent at his mercy and discovers that the Blaster is a retarded child. Having disobeyed the rules of the Thunderdome which demand a fight to the death, Max is banished to the desert where he is rescued by a tribe of wild children who are searching for a promised land. Together they rescue the Blaster from Bordertown and, while Jedediah prepares to fly the tribe to their new civilization, Max prepares resistance against Aunty's pursuing guards.

Once again one of the most immediately striking things about this latest *Mad Max* saga is its visual design. It is a world, according to production designer Graham Turner, that 'is absolutely low-tech – gritty lots of rust, with people just scratching and surviving on what they can.' Bartertown is a community designed out of junk, whilst the Thunderdome itself, a huge steel structure that spectators climb into to watch a fight to the death, is a sort of vast birdcage battle-field. As in the previous films, *Mad Max 3* evokes both ancient and modern worlds, on the one hand a futuristic fantasy but on the other, seeming more like a despoiled Biblical epic, with Max as Moses leading his children to the promised land. The epic associations are reinforced by the casting of Frank Thring (Pontius Pilate in *Ben-Hur* (1959) and Herod in *King of Kings* (1961)), in the role of Bartertown's collector.

There was always a satirical streak in the *Mad Max* films, but here it is bordering on self-parody. Nevertheless the jokes are good. When asked to shed his weapons for entry into Bartertown, Max takes a full minute to comply completely with the request. The duel to the death in Thunderdome is presented in the form

LEFT: *The Master Blaster, the all-powerful ruler of the Underworld. A curious creature consisting of a retarded dwarf called Master, astride the shoulders of a giant named Blaster, he is eventually befriended by Max.*

BELOW: *Aunty Entity, accompanied by her bizarre henchmen, pursues the errant Max into the desert beyond Bartertown.*

RIGHT: *Gibson and Bruce Spence in* Mad Max 3: Beyond Thunderdrome.

ABOVE: *Citizens of Bartertown gather for an evening's entertainment at the Thunderdome. Combatants (in this case Max and the Master Blaster), were expected to duel to the death.*

RIGHT: *Having disobeyed (and survived) the rules of the Thunderdome, Max was banished. He was saved from starvation in the desert by a tribe of feral children.*

of a game show ('Thunderdome live!'). Prior to the fight with the Blaster, Max is disarmingly told by the Dome's host: 'I know you won't break the rules – there aren't any.'

Prior to the film, Gibson was talking of its 'lifting the lid off the closet human being of *Mad Max 2*,' implying that there was to be more character development in this film. But this does not seem to be the case. Indeed in *Mad Max 3*, Max has become less of a figure of myth than a kind of eclectic hold-all of modern screen heroes. He is a rag-bag of cultural references, from Conan the Barbarian to James Bond (all gadgets and gimmicks), from the Man With No Name to Indiana Jones (the way to deal with a show-off is to shoot him). Max is not so much a character as a cartoon figure: Road-Runner more than Road Warrior. Perhaps it was this that prompted Mel to sound off against the film in the *People* interview. Indeed, Mel was more mad than Max: in the movie, he comes over as merely morose. Time for rest, retreat and recuperation, thought Gibson, after an exhausting year. The year's lay-off clearly recharged his batteries. He was to return more lethal than ever.

## CHAPTER 3

# THE BIG SHOT

'Any film which contrives to get both of its leading men stark naked within the first five minutes has a lot going for it. Danny Glover is no physical wreck, even when he's upped his real age by a decade to play a 50-year-old. But when your other piece of bare-ass is Mel Gibson, then you score *maximum* points.'

So wrote the critic Anne Billson, enterprisingly entering into the spirit of *Lethal Weapon* (1987), the movie that finally pitched Mel Gibson into the big league of modern film stars. Some doubts were voiced about the film's violence and vigilanti ethics, implicitly putting it alongside punchy movies like *The French Connection* (1971) and *Dirty Harry* (1971) as celluloid social commentaries on urban crime. But the merit of Ms Billson's raunchy insight is that she catches the tone of the movie, which is intended not as cinematic sociology but as a commercial crowd pleaser. It is basically a good guys – bad guys fantasy, decked out by director Richard Donner in the full-blown, mechanical overkill style of 1980s American cinema.

The twist in the formula is the central relationship between the two 'buddy' cops, Roger Murtaugh (Danny Glover) and Martin Riggs (Mel Gibson). It is a combustible contrast between black and white and between integrated Vietnam vet (Glover) and alienated Vietnam vet (Gibson). More specifically, it teams a middle-aged family man, who just wants to survive long enough as a cop to claim his pension, with a semi-psycho widower who enjoys playing Russian roulette with his life. The combination adds up to a sort of lethal Laurel and Hardy and, having set up its central premise, the film just lights the touch-paper and retires.

The plot begins with even more nudity than Ms Billson suggests. A topless call girl, high in more senses than one, falls to her death from a tower-block, victim of a lethal overdose of drugs. She turns out to be the daughter of one of Murtaugh's Vietnam buddies, Hunsaker (Tom Atkins), who asks him to find the killers. Martin Riggs is assigned as Murtaugh's partner. It turns out that the killers are ex-Vietnam mercenaries who have become drug traffickers, led by General McAllister (Mitchell Ryan) and his vicious albino sidekick Mr Joshua (Gary Busey). Hunsaker had been part of the set-up, and his daughter had been silenced to stop him from telling the police of his involvement. In the event, Hunsaker is shot and Murtaugh, his daughter Riane, and Riggs are captured by the gang. Riggs breaks free, rescues Roger and Riane, and eventually faces Joshua in unarmed combat.

The derivativeness of the plot is generally subsumed under the sheer energy of the film's style. To say the film is action-packed is something of an understatement: people fall through cars, buildings are blown up, there is a chase on a freeway, a karate fight, and a car even smashes through Murtaugh's front room (miraculously the house seems to have been repaired by the film's finale). But there is no doubt that what audiences really responded to was the volatile cocktail of Roger Murtaugh and Martin Riggs. From their 'meet-cute' onwards (when Murtaugh leaps on a scruffy individual in the police station who appears to be pulling a gun and is gently told that this is his new partner), the banter and the bravado never let up.

The film plays heavily on the contrast between the characters' domestic situations. Murtaugh's home scenes are cosy and sentimental enough to make even *The Cosby Show* look a bit austere. By contrast, Riggs' home is a

RIGHT: *One can almost hear the sharp intake of breath as thousands of fans look on in horror. A worrying moment from* Lethal Weapon.

ABOVE: *Gibson as Martin Riggs, the distraught and dangerous cop in* Lethal Weapon.

RIGHT: *Mel Gibson with Traci Wolfe on the set of* Lethal Weapon.

mess. Still distraught at the death of his wife in a car accident, Riggs is introduced to us through a haze of smoke, drinking and belching. Even his dog seems to disapprove of his lifestyle.

Some actors might have drawn back a little from the wilder excesses of the character, but Gibson relished the prospect of pushing it to even further extremes. 'I pictured Riggs as an almost Chaplinesque figure,' he said, 'a guy who doesn't expect anything from life and even toys with the idea of taking his own.' Riggs is not Dirty Harry, but Crazy Martin, and there seems to be a fine line between whether his madness is feigned or genuine.

This is particularly noticeable in two scenes. In one, he goes to talk down an intended suicide from a high building in a situation that seems lifted straight out of *Dirty Harry*, except in this case, Riggs handcuffs the man and then jumps with him. In the other scene with some drug dealers whom Riggs has set up, he disconcerts his adversaries by acting crazy to the point where they think he really is crazy. It is a scene that Gibson apparently semi-improvised, fluffing his hair and rolling his eyes to convince the druggies he is out of his mind. 'Shoot me, shoot me, shoot me,' he

repeats to the cops when one of the gang is holding him as shield. Is it a tactic to demoralize his captor, or is he really begging for death? It is a bit of business that is entirely appropriate to the character.

The fact that Gibson was allowed and encouraged to improvise in this way testifies to his close relationship with the director, Richard Donner, who was later to describe his star as 'a very special human being, the most exciting thing that's come into my life as an actor and a friend.' Indeed Gibson's contribution to the film might well have had an influence on the movie's style, encouraging it to go more bizarre and over-the-top. Certainly the final karate fight sacrifices all credibility in favor of exotic excitement, and Donner starts pumping up the wildness of the humor, like the moment when ultra-villain Joshua sprays bullets through a TV showing of *Scrooge* at the moment in the film when Scrooge has been converted to human goodness. Actor and director seem to feed off each other in this film, in a manner that was to be hugely profitable for both of them.

*Lethal Weapon* grossed over $100 million, so it was no surprise when the crazy cop duo were reunited for *Lethal Weapon 2* (1989),

ABOVE: *Murtaugh (Danny Glover) and Riggs (Mel Gibson), face another shoot-out. Part of the tension in* Lethal Weapon *derives from the contrasting characters of the duo.*

ABOVE: *The winning team of Murtaugh and Riggs returned in 1989 in* Lethal Weapon 2.

again directed by Richard Donner. The villains this time are a drug cartel operating from the South African Embassy, which gives them diplomatic immunity. As in *Lethal Weapon*, the villains are also a double-act: a super brain, Arjen Rudd (Joss Ackland) and his vicious sidekick Vorstedt (Derrick O'Conner). Also as in the previous film, an informer is threatening their operation, in this case an embezzling accountant (Joe Pesci) who is being offered immunity in return for evidence against the cartel. Assigned to protect the accountant, Riggs and Murtaugh become targets for what

one might call the South African connection.

Bugs Bunny was showing on Riggs's TV during *Lethal Weapon*, but this sequel is even more cartoon-like than its predecessor. The villains are comic-strip, and action verges on the gleefully absurd, notably when Murtaugh finds a bomb has been planted on his toilet, and must sit with his trousers down for 20 hours before his partner can help relieve the situation. The excesses reach delirious proportions when Riggs is making love to Rudd's conscience-stricken secretary Rika (Patsy Kensit) in his trailer, only for the home to be suddenly

ABOVE: *Gibson played the maverick cop, Glover the steady survivor. In this car chase scene, however, their usual roles seem reversed.*

LEFT: *Riggs begins to wish he'd tightened his safety belt before the truck moved off. Gibson at his most strenuous in* Lethal Weapon 2.

strafed and shredded by a helicopter attack initiated by Rudd. The BBC's Barry Norman wittily imagined the dialogue that might have followed this explosive event: 'Did the earth move for you darling?', 'Move? The whole house fell in!'

Actually the script (this time by Jeffrey Boam and not Shane Black) is not as sharp as that, and indeed in places seems unintentionally funny. A Negro cop listens to the most exaggerated Afrikaner voice on tape and says: 'Strange accent . . . I can't place it.' If all the cops are that slow, no wonder Riggs and Mur-

taugh are having to solve all the crimes on their own. There is a curious plot development when it emerges that Riggs's wife was actually murdered by Vorstedt, an opportunistic connection between the two films that seems more distracting than revealing. It is perhaps a sign of the times that the villains this time are not identified with Asia, or Southern or Central America, but with South Africa, whose apartheid attitudes are bluntly compared with those of Nazi Germany. Mel gets to do another of his bouts of virtuoso hysteria, as the action spirals into the surreal and almost supernatural in

total defiance of narrative logic.

*Lethal Weapon 2* was another box-office blockbuster. Reputedly it has grossed $300 million worldwide, which would please Gibson, as his contract entitles him to ten percent of the profits. There still surfaced, as with the first film, some liberal uneasiness about its ethical values. The villains were so hideously caricatured that an audience seemed invited to will their violent destruction: it was, some thought, the morality of the lynch mob and, as one critic said, it was the first time he had ever felt sorry for the South African government.

There was some perturbation too over the 'amorality' of the film – the tendency of our two trigger happy cops to shoot first and then read the corpses their rights – and over its allegedly excessive violence. Gibson robustly defended the film from such charges. He made a crucial, if controversial, distinction between the comic-strip violence of the *Lethal Weapon* films and the 'realistic' violence of a film like Sam Peckinpah's *Straw Dogs* (1972), a movie Gibson finds distasteful. *Lethal Weapon* is a fantasy, he said, recognized as such by the audience, popular because 'people like cowboys and Indians – that's basically what the film is.'

Sandwiched in between the mega-success of the *Lethal Weapon* movies was one of Mel Gibson's more obscure and most interesting films. In *Tequila Sunrise* (1988) he plays an ex-drugs dealer, Dale McKussic, who is in retirement in the South Bay area of Los Angeles and looking after his son on his own after the desertion of his wife. A narcotics agent, Maguire, (JT Walsh) suspects McKussic of still being involved in the drugs trade and is particularly suspicious of his regular frequenting of the Vellanari restaurant, believing that the owner Jo Ann Vellanari (Michelle Pfeiffer) might be a drugs connection. (In fact, McKussic frequents the restaurant so often because he is secretly in love with Jo Ann). A former friend of McKussic, now a cop, Nick Frescia (Kurt Russell) is assigned to investigate, and a complicated triangular relationship develops when he finds himself falling in love with Jo Ann whilst simultaneously trying to use her to frame his friend.

Events come to a head when a notorious Mexican narcotics dealer, Carlos, is expected to arrive to do a deal with McKussic. A crack Mexican drug enforcement agent Escalante (Raul Julia) is drafted in to assist in the surveillance and to help lay a trap. But Carlos and Escalante turn out to be one and the same and, moreover, a friend of McKussic's since they shared a prison cell in Mexico. There will be several more twists of bluff and doublebluff, tenderness and treachery to come before the drama is played out to the finish.

*Tequila Sunrise* is written and directed by Robert Towne, and catches a glossy and cynical 1980s materialism, where money talks louder than people, and feelings seem inextricably caught up in the cash nexus. It has a sweet smell of corruption and a touch of evil beneath the glamour. Everyone seems to be playing two roles, with desire apparently inseparable from deceit, and feelings caught up in the nets of manipulation. Which man does Jo Ann want? Is Frescia or McKussic intending to shoot the other at one stage: or McKussic and Carlos; or do they even know themselves? Even an order to cater for a birthday party is suspected of being a drugs transaction, a situation that McKussic is alerted to when, in classic Hitchcock fashion, he notices a dog-catcher is not catching a dog. It is a film about slippery friendships and treacherous alliances that may even extend to marriage: is McKussic really lying when he tells Carlos he will marry Jo Ann

BELOW: *Best friends since high school, Dale 'Mac' McKussic (Gibson) and Nick Frescia (Russell) have somehow ended up on opposite sides of the law. Quite how their relationship survived McKussic's career as a drug dealer and Frescia's employment as a police officer remains to be seen.*

because a wife cannot testify against her husband? Frescia conducts a romance with Jo Ann for subterranean business reasons, whilst McKussic is conducting business with her for subterranean romantic reasons. It is a film rich in enigma, achieving a fine balance between its character portraiture and its suspense structure. If the happy ending seems a miscalculation (one is glad Towne did not get his wish for a happy ending to his screen play for *Chinatown*), it nevertheless has its dark side and it may be that we are not meant wholly to believe it: wish-fulfilment more than dark reality.

The cast is splendid. Mel Gibson as usual projects a certain vulnerability behind a mask of self-reliance, an appealing uncertainty. As in a number of his films, though, he is at his most dangerous when his defenses are down and he is cornered like a bull in an arena: it is the moment when Carlos thinks him drunk and drugged that he can turn the tables on his friend. Michelle Pfeiffer is at her most sleekly stunning and that sometimes wooden performer, Kurt Russell, here excels himself, rising to the timing required in the lines and giving his role an appropriately complex charisma and charm. With the infallible Raul Julia also making his customarily expert contribution, it makes for a fascinating, almost Conradian exploration of the mystery of personality, and the complicated streams of trust and betrayal that flow through the closest human relationships.

Sadly, neither the critics nor the public liked *Tequila Sunrise* very much. Being an honest and self-critical performer, Gibson has himself confessed to not liking *Bird on a Wire*

RIGHT: *Mel Gibson with Arye Gross, who played his son in* Tequila Sunrise. *Deserted by his wife, Gibson's character gave up his life of crime to look after his son.*

ABOVE: *McKussic and Jo Ann Vallanari (Michelle Pfeiffer) endure a complicated relationship, the outcome of which only becomes clear at the end of the movie.*

LEFT: *Ever versatile, Mel is forced to supplement his income by working on a building site. A scene from* Tequila Sunrise.

ABOVE: *Mel Gibson and Goldie Hawn in* Bird on a Wire.

(1990) very much. Here he co-stars with Goldie Hawn, who encounters him at a filling station and recognizes him as her fiancé of 15 years previously who was supposedly killed in a plane crash. In fact he had had to go under-cover after being a prosecution witness in a drugs trial. Needless to say, the drug dealers he helped (or attempted to help) to put away are now after his blood. Naturally his ex-fiancée gets caught up in the chase and the two begin to rekindle the passion of that time long ago.

'There was a lot more promise in the script', said Gibson, 'Perhaps I didn't give it a good shot. I dunno, perhaps it's not my fault at all.' Although one can imagine Gibson as a laconic light comedian in a sort of George Segal mode,

he seems to be better at working comedy into a dramatic situation rather than playing it more obviously on the surface. Director John Badham (*Wargames, Short Circuit* and *Stakeout* among others) gives the movie his customary professional verve, but the narrative is episodic and strained. As a comedy thriller, it is neither comic nor thrilling enough: as is always the danger in this trickiest of genres, the two elements do not so much reinforce each other (as they do in Hitchcock) as cancel each other out. The film is probably at its best with its incidentals more than its essentials, like the moment when the hero attempts to fill in details of his past life for his ex-girlfriend while the two are edging their way across a high

ABOVE: *More an actor clinging helplessly to the side of a building, than a bird on a wire.*

61

LEFT AND FAR LEFT (BOTH): *In* Bird on a Wire, *Gibson played the long-lost fiancé of Goldie Hawn, a man who had apparently died in a plane crash 15 years earlier. His reappearance was not initially greeted with the overwhelming joy that may have been expected from his erstwhile lover, although she did help him escape from the underworld thugs who were hounding him.*

girder. It is comically incongruous but in its way dramatically appropriate – after all, given their situation, this might be the last chance he gets.

Gibson's next film, *Air America* (1990), turned out to be something of a disappointment too, though not for Gibson personally: he is reputed to have received a $7 million fee and also learned to fly a plane. A big budget movie shot over five months in Thailand and on sound stages in London, *Air America* tells the tale of an illicit weapons-for-drugs trade that was being carried out in Laos in 1969 with the tacit support of the CIA and US Army. Gibson plays Gene Ryack, a transport pilot for Air America (the name given to this operation) who is hoping this profitable gun-running will

soon enable him to settle down and retire with his Laotian wife and two children. Complications ensue, however, when he has to take responsibility for a new partner (Robert Downey Jr.). His collaboration with the operation is also put under scrutiny when he becomes involved with an aid worker (Nancy Travis) who is trying to help refugee villagers caught in the crossfire between the two sides.

The film is adapted from a book by the British journalist Christopher Robbins, a piece of thoroughly researched non-fiction. Curiously the 'Air America' operation is mentioned in *Lethal Weapon*, when Hunsaker, the father of the murdered girl, is explaining to Murtaugh how he became involved with General McAllister and his villainous drugs trade in the first place. 'I ended up working with a group called Air America. It was a CIA front,' says Hunsaker. 'They secretly ran the entire war out of Laos.' He goes on to tell of his involvement with Shadow Company, with a list of sources in Asia for shipments of heroin, 'all run by ex-CIA, soldiers, mercs . . . this is big business, Roger.' It might have been that connection that intrigued Gibson, as well as the fact, as he said, that it was an aspect of the Vietnam War that most Americans did not know about. 'In *Air America*,' Gibson said, 'we present the truth about war and business and how they are

ABOVE, LEFT AND FAR LEFT: Air America, *released in 1990, was a big-budget movie that provided the star with a change from the usual car chases. Gibson learnt to fly a plane in his role as transport pilot Gene Ryack, a man who is involved in a rather dubious gun-running operation in Laos in 1969.*

RIGHT: *Mel Gibson with Robert Downey Jnr., his co-star (and co-pilot) in* Air America.

FAR RIGHT AND BELOW: *Ryack is grounded by hostile forces somewhere in Laos.*

thought it was not hard-hitting enough, particularly disliking the characterization of the senator (Lane Smith) who is sent to inspect the operation in Laos. The film is trying to have it both ways, they argued: on the one hand, it purports to criticize this illicit operation but on the other, it ridicules the investigator of the corrupt trade.

The film's perceived confusion of purpose – is it a black comedy exposé or a fun action film, with serious undertones? – probably stems from a script that had been lying around so long that its original features were unrecognizable. It had been in development since 1978, had been rewritten three times, and had over the years picked up three different directors – Richard Rush (maker of *The Stunt Man*), Bob Rafelson (who had left the project to make *Mountains of the Moon*) and finally Roger Spottiswoode (ostensibly well cast, for he had made the brilliant 1984 political thriller, *Under Fire*, which had been critical of American foreign policy in Nicaragua). Finally the film was pitched between the anarchic antics of *M\*A\*S\*H* (1970) and the sentimental comedy of *Good Morning Vietnam* (1987).

As is his wont, Gibson consciously attempted to inject a bit more humor into the film. 'I thought it might be a better story if we lightened up on it a little bit,' he said. 'And it was lightened considerably.' However, it was not sufficient to make the film soar, either commercially or critically. By that time, though, he had something else on his mind. Indeed, when he came to do some post-production dubbing on *Air America*, he said, he found he was speaking some of his lines in iambic pentameter. What had intervened between the completion of *Air America* and his post-production work was the greatest challenge of Gibson's acting career to date: the title role in *Hamlet*.

inseparable. Somebody's getting rich, and it's always the wrong people.'

Was it a message movie, then? 'It doesn't hit you over the head,' says Gibson, 'nor should it. It's just there.' But it was a message that antagonized commentators on both sides of the political spectrum. Right-wing journalists queried its historical veracity. Left-wing journalists

## CHAPTER 4

# SOMETHING LIKE A DANE

The idea for doing *Hamlet* was first proposed to Mel Gibson while he was filming *Lethal Weapon 2*. His agent, Ed Limato, told him Franco Zeffirelli wanted to make the film and was wondering if Gibson would be interested in taking the main role. Actor and director met in a Los Angeles restaurant, talked for 12 hours about Shakespeare, and Gibson phoned the next day to confirm his acceptance of the role.

What had Zeffirelli seen in Gibson that caused him to think he was perfect for a Hamlet of the 1990s? Zeffirelli wanted Hamlet to be a 'virile, exciting, high-spirited man of the Renaissance.' For this he ideally needed an actor who was excellent on screen but who also had experience of performing Shakespeare on stage; who could combine the character's vital energy with his ironic humor; and, to get the film made, was a bankable box-office star. The only modern screen actor who measured up to all those requirements was Mel Gibson. Having watched him again in *Mad Max* and *Gallipoli*, Zeffirelli was more than ever convinced of his choice.

'It was a very big risk for him,' Zeffirelli has conceded. 'The scoffers are always waiting to blame people for ambition and longing to see them fall down. Mel has no reason to risk anything. He is one of the highest paid men on Earth. But he was prepared to put everything on the gambling table.' Certainly it could have been a disastrous acting and financial gamble for Gibson. Still, he probably thought he had a good hand. He had a director whom he trusted; who had cast Elizabeth Taylor in *The Taming of the Shrew* (1967), to the general mirth of the press, only for Taylor to confound the critics with a sparkling performance that upstaged that of her husband, Richard Burton. One suspects too that Mel relished the challenge and

felt he could succeed. 'Mel claims he is a barbarian tackling the Bard,' said his co-star Glenn Close, but he probably cultivated that as a fallback position in case the venture did not work. In fact, he had every reason to be confident. He was now a skilled and experienced film actor, and he had succeeded before in Shakespeare. It had all come together, he said, when he had played Romeo on stage and, as he put it, 'had developed a grasp of Shakespeare's language as the blueprint of something that could take motion and have a life distinct from the one it has on the page.'

Nonetheless, Hamlet remains a daunting prospect for any actor. Certainly, if he were to fail, thought Gibson, it would not be for want of preparation. He rented a house in Hertfordshire with his wife and six children and set to work. He gave up smoking, and practised swordfighting with Nathaniel Parker, who was to play Laertes in the film. He read countless critical commentaries on the role, to the point where even the ones that contradicted each other, he said, seemed equally plausible, so he put them to one side and concentrated on the text. For two months he had voice training from his voice coach Julia Wilson-Dickinson to master a classical English diction. The first read-through with the cast was nerve-wracking because he was confronted with a panoply of British theatrical talent, some of whom had done Hamlet themselves on stage: Alan Bates, Paul Scofield, Ian Holm. Yet they were all impressed by Gibson's dedication and his willingness to be guided by their experience. 'He's totally honest,' said Alan Bates. 'He can't emotionally tell a lie. He's completely centered on that.'

'I didn't find an accent until the first day of the shoot,' Gibson recalls. 'I noticed the value Ian Holm was getting from enunciating con-

RIGHT: *Is it a dagger he sees before him? Gibson confounded critics who predicted a farcical* Hamlet, *by delivering an excellent performance. Could more Shakespeare be forthcoming?*

sonants and I realized I was getting a little slack there. It was just a bad habit from American films where naturalism is emphasized to the nth degree.' Having settled on how Hamlet should sound, he then had to decide on how Hamlet should look. His hair was flattened down and lightly tinted, and he acquired a short beard. The slightly uncomfortable boots the wardrobe department had provided delighted him, because it gave him a walk that he felt was in character: the slightly jumpy, uneven gait of a man who is tense and not quite at ease with himself.

Zeffirelli's adaptation is textually quite bold. He cuts the opening scene entirely and, like Orson Welles' imaginative, eccentric film adaptation of *Othello* (1952), begins instead with the funeral of Hamlet's father, from which everything will flow. The King is mourned by Hamlet's mother, Gertrude (Glenn Close), and his uncle, Claudius (Alan Bates), who turns to Hamlet and says, ominously as it will turn out: 'Think of us as a father . . .' Zeffirelli also cuts the surrounding political context represented by the character of Fortinbras, whose aggression is usually seen as a dramatic contrast to Hamlet's hesitancy and delay. In Zeffirelli's reading, the narrative flows so quickly that

'delay' seems not to enter into it. For him, *Hamlet* is more a domestic than a political tragedy.

The emotional center of Zeffirelli's interpretation is Hamlet's feeling of betrayal by his mother. The dramatic heart of it stems from Hamlet's knowledge of a crime of which everyone else (except the killer) is ignorant. How to bring it out into the open? While working out how to expose the wrongdoer, Hamlet attempts to play with Claudius like a cat with a mouse – feigning madness, putting on an entertainment designed as a lethal weapon to incriminate Claudius before the whole court. For his part, Claudius keeps trying to outmaneuver Hamlet politically – sending 'friends' to spy on him, dispatching him to England with secret orders for his execution – until finally, in the duel scene, he gets too clever for his own good and the poison he has spread reaches himself. 'It's a great story', says Gibson, in the special 54 minute *Hamlet* video he made for American schools entitled, *Mel Gibson Goes Back to School*. 'There's something like eight violent deaths. There's murder, there's incest; there's adultery; there's a mad woman, poisoning, revenge, sword fights . . .'

Hamlet is a man in pursuit of revenge for psychological wounds of an emotional, fami-

ABOVE AND LEFT:
*Zeffirelli's* Hamlet *was carefully planned over a number of years. Several British castles doubled as Elsinore, and costume reflected the exigencies of medieval life in drafty rooms, rather than resorting to the traditional doublet and hose.*

lial nature, and to this end feigns madness and commits acts of sometimes appalling cruelty. This combination of manic action and private suffering could almost be a description of Mad Max or Martin Riggs. Small wonder that Zeffirelli thought of Gibson for his modern Hamlet, or that Gibson fits so snugly into the role. He gives a fresh, straightforward, effective performance. This is not an inner, poetic Hamlet. The soliloquies are relatively low-key and even informal, as if a thoughtful man is thinking on the wing, as it were, rather than an introspective poet is baring his soul, as is sometimes the approach. The 'To be or not to be' and even 'Alas, poor Yorick' speeches are handled with disarming directness, as if these thoughts are popping up inside the character's head for the first time and, in a way, taking him by surprise.

In the early scenes, one is less impressed perhaps by his speech as by his movement: restless but also furtive, an outward show of the character's inner disquiet. He is on the outskirts of the action, a pocket of black-clad disapproval in the initially cheerily colorful court, staring down in disdain at Polonius's advice to his daughter, or in disgust at Claudius's banqueting – keeping aloof, but missing nothing. As the drama develops, however, Gibson comes into his own with moments of flashing insight. He is particularly good in 'The Mousetrap' scene, the play-within-a-play for which he has devised a speech that he hopes will make evident Claudius's guilt. In his excited emotional state, he starts playing off Ophelia against Gertrude (the 'get thee to a nunnery' speech has been effectively and imaginatively transposed to this scene). As the performance builds to its explosive climax, he wanders among the audience in agitation. In a memorably observant touch, he mouths in silent imitation of the Player King the speech he has composed as the trap for Claudius, relishing the moment of his uncle's nemesis, almost tasting it on his lips.

He is equally striking in the duel scene at the end with Laertes, a contest that Claudius has contrived in order to kill Hamlet. Gibson begins to take risks as an actor, a sign in him not of nervousness or desperation but of increasing confidence. He begins particularly to highlight Hamlet's 'antic disposition' by playing the fool and winking at his mother. It is a display ingeniously in character, reflecting not only Hamlet's ironic humor but also his growing fatalism: he knows Claudius is plotting against him, he knows he is dancing with death. In this version, Claudius's messenger, Osric, played here by John McEnery, is no comic fop but seems an emissary of doom: also the weapons for the contest are not the usual fencing foils but much more lethal broadswords. One mistake and you can lose your head-literally.

Gibson has always been good at moments like these. They have occurred before in his work – his craziness with the drug dealers in

*Lethal Weapon*, his representation of Fletcher Christian's hysteria after the mutiny in *The Bounty* – where the character lets himself go, and you are unsure whether he is 'acting mad' to disconcert his adversaries or has genuinely lost control. This occurs in at least two other scenes in *Hamlet*. In his scene with Ophelia,

he suddenly spots shadows on the wall and realizes he is being spied on, so when he asks Ophelia the whereabouts of her father, and she replies, 'At home, my lord,' he knows she is lying. Is his subsequent eruption of anger a genuine outburst against female duplicity, or is it simply a performance of madness for the

RIGHT: *'Look here upon this picture . . . This was your husband . . .' (III:4) Hamlet confronts his mother with his feelings about her precipitate remarriage.*

benefit of the spies? Similarly in the great closet scene with Gertrude, Hamlet seems partly out of control but in another sense is quite calculatedly trying to stir his mother's conscience: in this version, when she kisses him to silence him (the incestuous emotions are very strong here), the Ghost reappears, one feels, to re- buke both of them. There is no doubt, then, that Gibson has been carefully cast for the film and rises to the challenge, offering more than enough to intrigue both students of Shake- speare as well as those of screen acting.

Gibson is supported by an excellent cast, with Alan Bates as a craftily avuncular Clau-

dius, Glenn Close a nervously neurotic Gertrude, Ian Holm a pompous and petulant Polonius, Paul Scofield an imposing Ghost and Helena Bonham Carter a genuinely moving Ophelia. As an interpretation, Zeffirelli's film perhaps lacks the personality and imagination of Olivier's 1948 *film noir* rendering, or the powerful political bleakness of Grigori Kozintsev's 1964 Soviet version. In contrast to Kozintsev's Soviet steel and Olivier's whiplash wit, Zeffirelli offers Italianate earthiness and heart-on-the-sleeve emotion. It is not subtle Shakespeare but it is gripping story-telling and sensual and suspenseful cinema. As such, it provides an admirable and appropriate con-

text for Gibson's performance, which in turn seems ideally attuned to Zeffirelli's articulate, no-nonsense interpretation.

The film has been a personal success for them both, but Zeffirelli has been the first to admit that the actor's triumph is more substantial than his. 'As a director,' said Zeffirelli, 'I can make a good, bad or mediocre film, and more or less remain the same. But if Mel did not pull out a convincing performance, he would have been crippled, not only artistically; he would have become a joke.' In fact, Mel has had the last laugh. He has played Hamlet – and won. And if he can play Hamlet, what can he not play?

BELOW: *'A hit, a very palpable hit!' (V:2) Gibson learnt to fence early in his career, although it was not a skill he needed until Hamlet.*

ABOVE: Lethal Weapon 3. *Gibson pictured with Danny Glover, Joe Pesci and Rene Russo.*

LEFT: *Gibson and Glover take on the bad guys in* Lethal Weapon 3.

After the completion of *Hamlet*, Mel retreated to his 600-acre cattle ranch in New South Wales (he has another one in Montana) to occupy himself for a while with cow management. He is a country boy at heart, some would say, and essentially a private man who thinks it wiser 'to marry out of your profession,' a family man who has striven to keep his wife and children out of the public eye. The family has always seemed to be as important to him as any career ambitions. He could even reflect with some equanimity on his decision to turn down the lead in one of the biggest box-office successes of recent years, *Ghost* (1990). 'It just didn't seem a very good part at the time,' he said. After *Hamlet*, he had probably had enough of ghosts.

But the public had certainly not had enough of Martin Riggs. In 1992, Gibson was re-united with Danny Glover in *Lethal Weapon 3*, again directed by Richard Donner. This time Riggs and Murtaugh are pitted against an ex-cop-turned-crook Jarvis (Stuart Wilson), whose trail they pick up after they have foiled a security van robbery that has been using special issue, armor-piercing bullets. After his breezy appearance as the police informer in *Lethal Weapon 2*, Joe Pesci is on hand once more to provide light relief. Indeed, what is noticeable about the new film is the increasing accent on comedy and explosive stunts in contrast to the character development and more logical narrative structure of the first film. Now that we know the characters, of course, the film does not need to take up much time with psychological exposition: it can simply deposit its heroes in one sensational set-piece after another.

Riggs this time is provided with a love interest in the form of a spunky Internal Affairs agent, Lorna Cole (Rene Russo). Also Roger Murtaugh, whose imminent retirement at the beginning of *Lethal Weapon 3* seems to provoke Riggs into ever more desperate and dangerous deeds, announces by the end that his retirement plans are shelved. The implication is that he is preparing himself for *Lethal Weapon 4* (certainly the worldwide success of the film seems to make another sequel inevitable). One suspects that the next film might get back to the original premise and provide some powerful motive for Riggs once again to immerse himself in his self-destructive element, which was the feature that attracted Gibson to the role in the first place.

There is a discernible pattern to Gibson's current career profile: a film for the action fans, a romance to appease his female following, and then, if possible, one to please himself. After the all-action *Lethal Weapon 3*, the romantic project was *Forever Young* (1992), directed by Steve Miner who has hitherto been most closely associated with *Friday the 13th*-type horror films. Gibson plays a test-pilot in 1939 who submits to being deep-frozen in a scientific experiment after his girlfriend has been in a car crash that has left her in a coma. Defrosted 50 years later by two boys, he goes in search of his true love. It sounds like a romantic stew, made up of ingredients from *Sleeper* to *Always*, from *Ghost* to *Back to the Future*. The film has performed strongly in America and has a fine supporting cast, headed by Jamie Lee Curtis and George Wendt.

Gibson's personal project is *The Man Without a Face* (1993), the film with which he will make his directing debut and also star. The material sounds intriguing and potentially risky, for Gibson plays a recluse who develops a friendship with a lonely boy but who has a dark secret in his past – namely, that he is an ex-con who has been indicted for child abuse. It appears to be something of a return to the emotional terrain of *Tim*, in which Gibson first demonstrated his sensitivity as an actor. It will be interesting too to assess his potential as a director and whether that is likely to mark a new direction in his career.

There is a nice line in Sergio Leone's epic, ironic western *Once Upon a Time in the West* (1969) when Jason Robards has watched Charles Bronson's harmonica-playing cowboy wipe out some especially hardened outlaws. 'He not only plays,' says Robards thoughtfully, 'he can shoot too.' Mel Gibson is not only a glamour film star of a kind barely seen since the 1930s: he can act too. 'Barely seen,' though, might be an apposite phrase. He has been quoted as saying that 'if I've still got my pants on in the second scene, I think they've sent me the wrong script.' Amusement, or a sign of frustration? Is there a feeling, even after *Hamlet*, he is still not taken seriously enough as an actor? Some of his best screen acting – in *The Year of Living Dangerously, Mrs Soffel, Tequila Sunrise* – has been in some of his least popular films. Perhaps the most fascinating question about his immediate future is the success with which he might be able to pull together three of the main guiding lights of an actor's career: audience, ambition, awards.

However, there is no need to worry, or hurry. He has still several years to go before he is 40. He has enormous potential still to be tapped. As one of the biggest contemporary stars and with a track record that ranges successfully from *Mad Max* to *Hamlet*, there seems no limit to what he still, excitingly, might achieve.

ABOVE: *Gibson and Isabel Glover in* Forever Young.

LEFT: *Gibson befriends Elijah Wood in* Forever Young.

# INDEX

Figures in *italics* refer to illustrations

## Acknowledgments

The author and publisher would like to thank the following for their help in the preparation of this book: Alan Gooch the designer, Pat Coward for the index, Nicki Giles for production, Damian Knollys for editorial assistance and Judith Millidge for editing it.

All of the photographs were provided by the Brompton Picture Library except for the following:
Photofest pages 77(both) 78, 79(both)
Smeal/Gallela Ltd page 5